Meditatio Placentae

Meditatio Placentae

poems by Monty Reid

Brick Books

Library and Archives Canada Cataloguing in Publication

Reid, Monty, 1952–, author
   Meditatio placentae / Monty Reid.

Issued in print and electronic formats.
ISBN 978-1-77131-439-8 (paperback).—ISBN 978-1-77131-441-1 (pdf).—
ISBN 978-1-77131-440-4 (epub)

   I. Title.

PS8585.E603M44 2016   C811'.54   C2015-907891-1
                                       C2015-907892-X

Copyright © Monty Reid, 2016

We acknowledge the Canada Council for the Arts, the Government of Canada through the Canada Book Fund, and the Ontario Arts Council for their support of our publishing program.

The author photo was taken by Pearl Pirie.
The book is set in Sabon.
Design and layout by Marijke Friesen.
Printed and bound by Sunville Printco Inc.

Brick Books
431 Boler Road, Box 20081
London, Ontario N6K 4G6

www.brickbooks.ca

For FMR

CONTENTS

Household Gods 1
Frances Disassembles the Pop-up Book 15
Site Conditions 19
Lost in the Owl Woods 29
Meditatio Placentae 37
So Is the Madness of Humans 47
A Poem That Ends with Murder 57
Moan Coach 67
Contributors' Notes 81

Acknowledgements 91
Biographical Note 93

Household Gods

1. Sock

A basket full of the tongues of liars
still warm from the dryer
dozes on the table.

In the warmth of their sleep
they call softly for their lost mates.

Always, they want to find the one true
image of themselves, their only
lint, their only static.

Which is why few things are sadder
than a single sock at the bottom
of the basket,

a sock no one will wear again.

2. Lint

Every night a deep spring
fills the small pool of my navel.

In the soft hours all the thirsty animals
come down to drink.

You can never see them
but you can tell they were there

because the grass has been trampled
all around the pool

and the flocks of lesser hungers
are grooming themselves quietly in the trees.

That's the way it is
with the grey hours and the reliable animals.

Once you've fed them
You're stuck with them.

3. Kleenex

The folded tears
have multiplied
in their box.

When you let
one of them out
all the others

try to get out too.

4. Tweezers

At the far, hard end
of their existence

these two old friends
cannot do without each other.

But today they are not speaking.

Something has come between them.
And now it's gone.

5. Button

A small white button
lying in the corner.

I remember how your blouse
was undone.

A small white button
with two eyes wide open

as if surprised.

6. Keys

Someone took the keys
from the drawer where
they multiplied when
no one was looking.

Who knows what they will open
now. When they are left
undisturbed on the counter

their carefully cut teeth
line up with the kitchen's
magnetic fields.

Wherever they point
there is a door.

7. Pillow

As I lay awake I could hear wings
as the angular geese swept up the valley

in the clarity of an October night.

Would it not be akin to grace, to be
unfolded like this by the rushing air?

Of course the pillow can be folded.
Of course the air rushes by.

8. Chair

The chair is what's left after you sit in one place
long enough.

This one, all that remains from an old kitchen set,
is painted white

like a skeleton, like the hard evidence
of waiting,

proof
that the waiting is over.

It is a simple chair. It has waited
that long.

9. Pick

The corners get worn off, in a characteristic pattern
by which you can tell

how the instrument was held
and the angle by which the strings were struck.

This is how the music was made.
The more it is used

the less it looks like itself.
The more music that is made

the sooner it needs
to be replaced.

10. Cork

It lies on the counter, punctured
at one end
and stained at the other.

It held out as long as it could.
It saved us from the wine
for a couple of days, anyway,

and now there is nowhere
to go back to.

11. Security Light

Something irresistible arrives out of the darkness.

It draws the sprinklers from their burrows
and nuzzles the intricate cones of the lilacs.

Unoccupied cars stir briefly as it passes.

Voices were arguing
somewhere down the street

and the security light clicked on again, off again,
imagining someone was there.

12. Upright Bass

The night after my wife bought her new bass
I lay in the upstairs bed as she practiced an old
song called *Travellin' Blues*.

It was a second-hand bass, and she said
it was so big it felt like she was waltzing with someone
she didn't know.

Her hip was already bruised
because she kept nudging the reinforced edges
towards her particular sense of rhythm.

When she finally came to bed, with
her bruises and blisters and taped-over fingers,
I was sleeping. I was dreaming

about stepping on her toes.

13. Shirts

There was a cool spring breeze and she had washed his shirts
and hung them outside to dry.

He was working at his desk when he noticed movement
just beyond his vision.

First he thought someone was coming to the door
but when he looked again those shirts made him feel

strangely empty, as if he was out there
blowing around in the April wind.

Late in the afternoon she gathered them in,
pressing them for a moment to her face,

taking in that crisp but unmistakable smell
of no one.

14. Printer

Begins printing at midnight.
No one is at the computer. A light snow is falling.
There are still ashes glowing in the fireplace.
And then the printer starts up.

I've been suspicious for a while
that the words aren't mine.
A sequence of small lights
that replace the losses.

I don't know what I expected
as I shivered in the dark room
and the paper filed through the slot.

More than one copy
and each one, lyrics
of a song sung by EmmyLou Harris
although she didn't write it.

Frances Disassembles the Pop-up Book
For John Lavery

1.

The contrary garden
survives on spit and drool.

Pretty maids
have their corners folded over.

There is one monosyllabic row
of them
left

and still, they make the action
happen.

2.

The next page is Jack Be Nimble.
If we tear off the image of the candlestick

behind which the mechanics
and the slots for the mechanics
are apparent

then
a fire burns
somewhere else.

Where no one is jumping.

3.

We would prefer to chew the page
where the big spider
emerges

out of the architecture of the thick stock
into the world.

There is a history of teeth marks on Miss Muffet
but she remains functional.
So far.

4.

Around they go on the magic disc.
Ring around the rosie.

The rabbits dance
then get bent out of shape
in this pastorale.

No, you're supposed to turn it
not bend it.

The way the new moon has an arc
where your finger will just fit

and the rabbits probably
proliferate upon it.

5.

The teeter
totters

not with
your daughters

or your sons.

The teeter
tatters

not with your teeth
but with your gums.

6.

The cows are in the corn

and we have pulled down the flap
on the haystack so often
it just stays down.

The sun that pops up
above the gleaming meadow
has been ripped, almost, from the page.

This is your favourite part.
Where you have found everything
there is to find, almost,

and keep on looking.

7.

Look.

First they get the water
then they tumble.

Down the hill.

What could we have done to prevent this,

sweetie?

What have we done
to the ones we love?

8.

In the final scene
all the materials of the night sky

pop up and twinkle.
They are anxious to meet you.

The picket fence pops up.

The damaged animals at the window
of the unfolded house

are looking up.

At least they think it's up.

Site Conditions
For Barry Padolsky

1. Crane

Deus ex machina.

A claw comes out of the sky.

2. Cement Truck

In the origins of cement
there is always a truck.

It waits at the curb
turning on its axis.

Sometimes it is full, the story goes
and sometimes it is empty.

After that
it's cement all the way down.

3. Bobcat

It keeps its brain in a cage
for safety reasons.

Even so, its mouth
is always the first thing there.

4. Hard Hat

It's hard to look up
so you never know what's falling.

But whatever falls
never hurts you.

5. Torch

What the fire destroys
the fire can also heal.

Either way, never
look at the flame.

6. Scaffold

We built this inattentive structure
out of insect legs and wind

so you can't see what we're working on.

When we take it down
we'll be gone.

7. Glove

One glove is lost.

The other one says, Hold on to me
hold on to me.

It knows.

8. Pallet Jack

Put your hand under
and lift.

Not there

there.

9. Pipe

If all the pipe in the world was laid end to end
it would reach to where, Mars?

That's what pipe dreams of, lying there in a pile.

Much later, you will hear them in the walls.
Complaining, always complaining.

10. Chop Saw

Measure twice
and cut once is what they say.

Just cut, I say
just cut.

11. Cable

It finds a way
through the maze
of what you knew.

Whoever comes behind you
will wonder where the hell
you were going.

12. Architect

The architects are on site
with their hard hats and smartphones.

This was supposed to be a bridge, they say.
This was supposed to be a temple.
This was supposed to be obvious.

And now, the architects are gone.

13. Ladder

Whatever takes you up
also carries you down.

You will have to go
the way you fear the most.

14. I-Beam

In cross-section
it is pure ego.

If you cut it there
it won't hold anything
up.

15. Insulation

The cold stays out
the dreams stay in.

It has an itch
so you don't have to.

16. Barrel

No one knows what's inside.

Someone has taken a deep breath
and is holding it

until you're gone.

17. Drywall

If it is all surface
then there's nothing behind it.

I never lied to you
it whispers

to all
the disappointed nails.

18. Flatbed

No, I want the enormous
truck.

I mean the really big truck.

The big one.

For chrissakes.

19. Trouble Light

They kept the light
in that little cage
all afternoon.

No wonder it's gone.

20. Brush

They're painting now.
That means they're almost done.

You missed a corner
over there.

Lost in the Owl Woods
For SKH

1.

A woman in a long coat climbs into a tree.
To an observation platform at the edge of the woods.

The trails disappear
and what holds up the rickety constructions?

Muffled light
comes and gets her.

A long coat makes it hard to climb.

She believes in observation.
It's cold.

2.

A woman in a long coat
watches a history of the fields.

Loose wire at the edges.

Earlier, an owl made of snowlight paced her,
flying from post to post as she skirted the woods,
finally scooping a vole from the trail
right in front of her.

Hunger is a loose wire.

3.

A woman in a long coat
stands on the observation platform
and puts on her binoculars.

Wings
unbundled into the restricted light.
Focus, just focus

and it could be the sharp edges
of your life
close enough to touch.

4.

On the observation platform there is room for one at a time.

She doesn't trust it
but it holds her.

5.

The woman in the long coat is in the owl woods
and it's getting dark.

She pulls her scarf down from her ears
and stands still,

thinking for a moment that there was some sound
other than her own,

but it doesn't repeat.

Still,
it was there.

6.

The woman in the long coat
knows there is a way out of the owl woods

if you turn around.
But the snow is falling
and the tracks are gone.

And what turns around
is gone.

She tucks what is left of the light
around her

and climbs down from the observation platform
one careful step
after another.

7.

The woman in the long coat
has walked deep into the owl woods.

She is humming a small song to herself
because she is afraid
and happy.

The owls tilt on their platforms.
The light is perfect.

Meditatio Placentae

1.

I came out too, with just as much necessity but none
of the adoration. I have to assume the world will contain us.

Not the mother, or the child, but something unembraceable
and always between this place and another.

The midwife took me in her gloves and spread me on the cold tray.
She said I was complete, but that has never been true.

Even now, I want the rest of me to show up
and be similarly loved.

2.

I never asked for the needle either, no matter how enhanced it was
with its minute corrugations so it shows up better on the ultrasound

and still, it doesn't know what it's looking for.
It slides through my expanded cells, through the apart of surfaces

and tastes the order of what will disappear. All
good flesh will. But what it wants, now, is just a sample

of the fluids, the ones that focus the attention and amplify
the repetitive heart. If we could see, we could see

through it. I never asked for anywhere else
and yet every somewhere else is within me.

And when I threaten to detach
it's gone.

3.

When the time comes, the broken water disappears
into the seam of itself, and then the carry-on full of small bones

articulated as an I will also disappear.
They will be expecting me then.

And what would be the point of hanging on?
Just to be the lining of belief, after belief itself is gone?

Put it to music, I say.
Already I can hear the wailing.

4.

I came out, and it is the going out that still concerns us, with a kind of
plop, not exactly the celestial soundtrack all the attendants

in their hospital gowns expected. And for a while, I am in and out of
the body, like the soul escaping in one of those voluptuous old paintings

with angels instead of midwives, but with the same drapery.
They were supposed to examine me, but with all that bright light

and finery, who can blame them for a certain distraction.
The body always retains something of what it gives up,

a trace of what's gone. But of course the body has also been given up
by something with different audio. I came out with a kind of plop

and then there was another but less emphatic plop when they
dropped me in the yoghurt tub, so the angels can carry me back home.

5.

Typical, they put the baby in a sling and planted the prickliest tree
they could find to celebrate her birth. A hawthorne.

According to some, it's a contraindication for vampires.
To others, it made the crown of thorns Christ wore on the cross

and sometimes it still groans with the guilt and bureaucracy.
Or it marks a door to the world of faeries and preternatural births.

They don't believe any of that shit and were in such a distracted rush
when they planted the tree they forgot to throw me in the hole

and early next morning had to go and get me out of the freezer
and do it over again.

They defrosted me in the microwave
but at least they didn't try to eat me, like some people do.

6.

After all that fuss
how could they think I'd leave nothing behind,

that I would fall onto the wet sheets,
onto the soak of light without regrets,

without a trail – of clots, of repeats, of fragile genomes –
to follow back home.

The midwives were wrong and careless
and I was bound to forget.

But what is forgotten must also exit the body
and the unscraped languages it is put together with.

Dilate the passage. Curette the pieces.
Spoon-feed the hungry world.

7.

Six weeks postnatal
and she was bleeding onto the floor at the triage desk in the Montfort

and the doctor who saw her eight hours later sent her home at two a.m.
saying she just had gotten her period unusually early.

Still bleeding, she came back the next day
but it took another five hours and an ultrasound to determine

there was a problem and even then it wasn't until she had bled through
all the bedclothes and her hemoglobin level had fallen past critical

that they concluded there was reason to respond.
They had to scrape the so-called products of conception

from the uterine walls, and after, they stood at her bedside
and congratulated themselves for catching it just in time.

That's what I was. A product of conception.
I learned that those who cause the greatest pain have the kindest voices.

I never wanted to know
and never expected to be human.

8.

So, finally I have been removed.
Whatever it is that remembers, can stop now.

Elsewhere
oozes into the hawthorne.

Whose eyes are those?
What is an open in the body?

No one will look for resemblances.
I will resemble, nonetheless, all of you.

9.

Reroute the blood and detach the wings.
What things still need me.

I always come after.
I abandoned the bodies of the living.

I did not want the sentence to finish.
But it finished anyway.

So Is the Madness of Humans
For Rob MacInnis

1. Dress Rehearsal

The madness of animals is to think that they're human.
So is the madness of humans.

The madness of animals is way ahead of the madness of humans.
So is the madness of humans.

The madness of animals comes in through little holes cut
in all the surfaces, just like the madness of humans.

More animals are coming. Their faces have been processed
to let the whole world in. So is the madness of humans.

2. Opening Night

They are waiting for you to appear.
There is space for you in this theatre of light.

The space you have entered is unreal space
but is the only space where the animals can see you.

You are bearing the signals they have been waiting for.
The signals of light-emitting objects too far away

to be remembered by anything but the camera.
Sit down in front where they can see you.

3. Farm Family

They are in the failing structures, but they aren't here.
They are in the wrecked vessels, but they aren't here.

The spooks of light all look like animals to me.
They are waiting for your response, somewhere else.

They have emerged outside of us and perch in the chemicals.
The chemicals have always been clear about it.

I used to have someone to miss.
And when I close my eyes the animals are there.

4. Fresh Faces 1

Look how you looked before, I tell them.
How's that, I asked.

Undiscovered, I tell them.
Don't preen, I tell them.

There is the coursing of blood.
There is the pose of the wind.

And then I became a fish, I tell them.
It could happen to you.

5. Fresh Faces 2

They have gathered together to watch tv.
This is the only bar around with a big screen.

You want to talk to them
as if discourse was more important than good hands.

They don't cheer for the same team as you.
They know language is a bad contract.

Shut up and watch the game, they say,
again.

6. Angelina

When you see the photograph you touch your own face absentmindedly. Yes, of course it's you.

Stop talking about the face as if it was just some category.
Stop talking about the face as if it was empty.

Only the privileged think the subject would exclude us.
Only the privileged want to keep on talking.

True, the light of countless stars roams in your eyes.
And now it wants out.

7. Rhode Island

Don't you recognize me?
In all the zones of probability.

In all the temptations of space.
Don't you recognize me?

In the dark space where things cannot be put.
Don't you recognize me now?

There was something I forgot to do. I was
supposed to count how many of you there still were.

8. Untitled 1

They are staring into your room.
Like all the rest of the photographs did.

After all, what does any image need but more room.
Or nudes, maybe.

No. No nudes.
An image needs more room.

Yours.
Take your clothes and leave, now.

9. Rachel

The absence of evidence is not in the photograph.
The evidence of absence is not in the photograph.

Yes, we were lovers a long time ago. It's true,
that shot doesn't do justice to your beauty.

But always
you have to work with what you've got.

I'll be here watching.
Call me.

10. Untitled 2

The light is full of questions.
Where were you? When?

Move over where the eyes were
and let us get a good look at you.

The pain of the body running out of its own presence
can be managed these days.

Yes, you're guilty.
You were guilty from the start.

A Poem That Ends with Murder

1.

He is building a narrative with constricted air
and a room abandoned by everyone else.

There is the affectionate fauna of his breath
to keep him company.

He has told the same story before
with its gaps and false starts and underdeveloped plot
and yet all he can do is keep telling it.

2.

Some people dream, but he has been banished
from the dream world.

Instead, sprites and angels that guard the entry
reach for their earplugs and turn away.

It has gotten so that he is turned on by their backs,
the moles and curves and the inconsistent vertebrae.

That too has become part of his story.
He thinks the deaf could love him
but damned if they'll listen.

3.

He awoke one night with a thumb and forefinger
pinched over his nose.

And once with a pillow over his face.

And once with a knee in the back
– okay, more than once.

Once there were kids setting off fireworks in the park.
And once with sirens blaring outside.

Even in his sleep
what he wants is an audience.

4.

In the part of the brain that is active
when he sleeps

primitive jealousies light up.
It's just as well no one can see them.

Tho he is worried about the faint glow
that seems to come from the base of the skull

when he wakes up in a sweat,
his arm around the remaining pillow.

5.

The confession is suctioned out of him
at length, every night.

Yes, I did it.
It feels better to tell someone.

But there's more.

There is something that confesses to him,
that ratchets its little amours

into his breath every night,
that says, yes, yes

I did it too.

6.

It's worst when he lies on his back.
When he's facing the darkness
with his lopsided nose and exposed genitalia
and the darkness keeps saying,
We can't hear you . . . what is it you want?

But it's also bad
when he lies curled up on his side
in the favorite position of the species
and although there is no one to snuggle with
there is, nonetheless, the same question.
And the same, if somewhat muted, attempt to answer.

The only possible relief
comes when he sleeps on his belly.
Whatever is going on happens behind him
and they just take one look at that hairy ass
and don't even ask.

7.

Lately, it's gotten so bad
that he's snoring even before he falls asleep.

The heavy book falls from his hand ... he snores
... then his head drops. In that order.

Then, and this is the saddest thing,

he wakes up and looks around
to see if anyone noticed.

8.

When he tried the device given to him
by the dentist, it was like having another mouth
inside the one he thought was his.

The new mouth never says what he expects it to say.
But then, neither did the old one.

9.

Once, we had to stay in the jacuzzi room at the Moulin Rouge Motel
because our campsite got flooded and that was the only room
left in town. It was soooo bad. He eventually slept out in the truck.

Well, once we had to stay in a lot of places and there's
no point in complaining about them
now.

In fact, after a while complaining just starts to sound
like nostalgia.

Once, we had to stay in this little panza in northern Hungary
and in the middle of the night, just so everyone could sleep,
he had to sneak off into another room, which was, luckily, both vacant
and unlocked.

But the hostess found him the next morning and although he wanted
to pay for the extra room she was laughing too hard to take his money.

The breakfast sucked though.

10.

The more he tried to stay awake the more tired he became.
Well ... what would you expect?

Since he could not dream he came to love
his snoring, claiming that it was equally
the working out of a problem the conscious mind
couldn't solve.

He even claimed, in his expansive moments,
and in the face of some contrary evidence,
it was a kind of song, an attempt
to sing into being whatever was in his head.

She was unconvinced.

She said, The only way this will end will be with murder.

Moan Coach

1.

She was asked to be part of a production of *The Vagina Monologues*
but after a couple of rehearsals they said she wasn't convincing enough.

Convincing enough at what, she thought?
It's your moan, they said, it needs some work.

You have to moan as though you aren't doing it for an audience.
You're going to need some help.

2.

The long gloss of winter lay over them.

They made love that night and her partner stopped
and leaned back on her elbow and said, Are you thinking
about somebody else?

No, she said, I'm practicing.
I'm practicing not thinking about anyone.

3.

I don't know how to moan
and I don't know how not to moan either.

Is that me making that noise when your lips finally reach my breast?
I don't know what my own voice sounds like.

Inadequate, I guess, now that I'm paying attention.

But kiss me,
kiss me there again.

4.

But even with all that practice they still didn't like her moan
so they gave her a number to call.

It was some guy who'd coached the voices of stars
and made them all sound like they meant it.

Let's hear your moan, he said, and she tried.
I've heard better, he said.

So they worked at it for a couple of hours
and she sounded progressively alien to herself

and finally threw her hands up in – what was it?
hopelessness?

That's more like it, he said.

5.

It's getting better, they said at rehearsal.

You've changed, said her partner,
is there someone new?

Only me, she said,
only me
and my cold feet.

6.

Ah, he said, don't think of it as you.
It'll freak you out.

It's just a door opening into something.
You can go down the steps whenever you want
and disappear.

Only the words turn to look behind them.
Because they know they'll have to find their way back up again.

Jeesus, she said,
you're supposed to be helping me.

7.

Okay, then
think of it this way.

A moan doesn't come back.

8.

At the exact limits.
Words don't.

He recorded her and they listened to the file.
But it didn't sound like her, not even when it stopped.

In fact, nothing sounded like her any more
when it stopped.

Try again, he said.

9.

She was sleeping poorly.

Something gathered in the corners of the ceiling,
abandoned skins under the bed.

For sure there was all that moaning.
Yes, you were doing it again last night, said her partner.

I'll be in the spare room when you want me.

10.

It was tired, but somehow she was always
ready for another rehearsal.

And her moan now was an appeal that came from
somewhere outside anything that could be called her voice.

But by then it didn't matter.
To matter all sound would have to call to itself

and it doesn't.

11.

The stage lights were bright
but the floor was cold and her feet were freezing every night.

So she went to bed with the hot water bottle
which snuggled and gurgled against her

and in the morning it still held some residual heat
until she held it upside down above the sink and let the water out.

What was it she heard
as it emptied, then lay exhausted on the counter?

No, she thought, no
it wasn't.

12.

A moan is what happens
when someone else passes through the space
you are finished with.

The way things drift away to make room for the new claim
even though it said it didn't need much room.

The way you can still hear people talking
for a few minutes in the theatre after the lights go down

and the moaning hasn't started yet.

13.

When the show was over, and the reviews were in
and everyone commented, among the champagne
and well-toned glitter, on how much fun she seemed to be having
she said, I owe it all to my moan coach.

There were a few raised eyebrows
since no one except her ex knew what she was talking about
and even then, they thought the dimensions
of her voice were hers alone.

Ah, they said,
someone taught you how to do that?

Yes, she said, everybody did.

Contributors' Notes

1.

Monty Reid always reads the contributors' notes first. Before he even looks at the rest of the magazine. He has become interested in how people imagine themselves. Perhaps he has come to believe that these notes are more dynamic, more provocative, more disturbing even, than the poems.

2.

There are morning glories in the garden, growing up among the tomatoes. He likes them, but the deer don't. What deer? What tomatoes, for that matter.

3.

Monty Reid is an Ottawa investor. His favourite part of *The Globe and Mail* is the financial section. He likes the "Stars and Dogs" piece, where stocks are given quick and funny assessments. He sees them as haiku. Nobody else is credited, so he is quick to claim them for himself.

4.

When it comes to books, Monty Reid prefers the acknowledgements. He likes that they have gotten longer. There are just that many more people involved. He counts how many of them he knows.

5.

Monty Reid has poetry forthcoming in a number of magazines, both print and online. He can't remember which ones. He lives in Ottawa. Yes, he lives in Ottawa.

6.

Monty Reid likes it when contributors include some cute non-literary factoid about themselves. Like when someone lives with three cats, or plays guitar and mandolin in the band Call Me Katie. Ah, he used that one already.

7.

Writing as George Bowering, Monty Reid has published almost a hundred books. Many of them have won awards. He was in the air force for a while.

8.

Monty Reid writes in the basement. There is a book about parasites on his desk. His next publication will be called *Host*. The charger for his cellphone is also on his desk, but the phone is misplaced.

9.

Once an editor told him that he could never be a poet with a name like Monty. Once Bill Mitchell told him he couldn't play the piano either. They knew, apparently.

10.

Monty Reid writes in the morning, and gardens in the afternoon. There are aphids on the basil, and on the Brussels sprouts. He isn't worried about the Brussels sprouts.

11.

Monty Reid wasn't always this way. He used to browse through each new issue, reading what caught his eye, going back to reread pieces, often reading through the entire contents. Now, sadly, sometimes he never gets past the contributors' notes.

12.

Monty Reid is distantly related to Blaise Pascal, who said the last thing one settles in writing a book is what one should put in first. Monty Reid thinks contributors' notes should be placed before the poems, not after them.

13.

Monty Reid, is he still alive?

14.

No. Contributors' notes should be short and pithy.

15.

The stump of a huge black walnut tree is taking up space that could be a garden. Monty Reid has placed a bird feeder on the stump, but it isn't the same.

16.

Monty Reid doesn't know anyone anymore. That's one theory. The other is that he knows too many people. Either way, he doesn't know them.

17.

Monty Reid is best known for his translations from the Spanish. His expansions of Machado are used in schools throughout Castille, and his exquisite rewrite of Lorca is forthcoming from a Granada publisher. He was assassinated in 1936.

18.

The most annoying thing at a poetry reading is the poet. Monty Reid's most recent collection of poetry destroys the comfortable notions of personal identity decried and then rehabilitated by postmodernism.

19.

Monty Reid has new work in *Arc, Dusie, elimae, ottawater, New American Writing, Lana Turner*, and *Descant*, among many others. He still lives in Ottawa.

ACKNOWLEDGEMENTS

"Meditatio Placentae" first appeared in *The Malahat Review*. Parts of "Household Gods" first appeared in *Prairie Fire*. "Site Conditions" appeared in *ottawater* and as a chapbook from Apt. 9 Press. "Contributors' Notes" appeared in *Peter F. Yacht Club*, then as a chapbook from Gaspereau Press. "Lost in the Owl Woods" appeared in *The Fiddlehead* and as a handmade chapbook by artist Roberta Huebener published by BookThug. "So Is the Madness of Humans" was commissioned by the School of the Photographic Arts of Ottawa to accompany The Farm Family Project, an exhibition of photographs by Rob MacInnis. "A Poem That Ends with Murder" appeared as a chapbook from Apt. 9 Press. "Moan Coach" appeared as a chapbook from above/ground press. "Frances Disassembles the Pop-up Book" first appeared in *Grain*.

Thank you to the editors, curators, and producers involved. Thanks also to the Ontario Arts Council for a Writers' Reserve grant that assisted in the preparation of this book. Thank you as well to everyone at Brick Books – it's a pleasure to work with you again. And to Sarah Hill, my best reader and best friend, thanks for your patience and unflagging support.

MONTY REID is an Ottawa writer. His recent publications include *Garden* (Chaudiere Books, 2014) and *The Luskville Reductions* (Brick Books, 2008), as well as many chapbooks from Apt. 9, Gaspereau, above/ground, corrupt, Red Ceilings, and other small presses. He has won the Stephan G. Stephansson Award three times, the Archibald Lampman Award, two National Magazine Awards, and has been nominated for the Governor General's Award for Poetry on three occasions. He is the Managing Editor of *Arc Poetry Magazine* and the Director of VerseFest, Ottawa's international poetry festival.